The Altamont Fair
Bringing City and Country together with Tradition since 1893

Souvenir Edition

Don Rittner

Copyright 2022 by Don Rittner

All rights reserved. International copyright secured. No part of this book may be reproduced, stored in a retrieval system, or transmitted in any form or by any means electronic, mechanical, photocopying, recording, or otherwise—without the prior written permission of New Netherland Press and Don Rittner, except for the inclusion of brief quotations in an acknowledged review.

ISBN-13: 978-0-937666-55-5

Book design by Don Rittner

New Netherland Press
Schenectady, NY

First Edition

Dedication

To all the volunteers and staff that have made the Altamont Fair a success each year from 1893-2018.

Acknowledgements

The book was made possible thanks to the many people and organizations that took or donated photographs, and archived news clippings and other memorabilia about the fair over the last 125 years.

The many images found throughout the book are from individuals and collections that can be identified to a photographer and include Betty Zadora, Ev Rau, Mefford Photo, Ken Gypson, El Roth, JA Glen, John Papp, Jack Pollard, Edward Carpenter Brandow, Eddie Russo, Harold Han, Henry Sollman, Diana J Roberts, Warren F. Hockaday, Vicki Weagley, Brea-Anne Garahan, Marijo Dougherty, Gina Verrelli. Thank you Sue Clark.

This includes institutions such as the Schenectady Museum Archives, Chris Hunter, Cindy and, Village of Altamont Archives & Museum, Melissa Hale-Spencer, editor, Tim Albright, The Altamont Enterprise & Albany County Post; The Edwin Bradt Collection, the Altamont Enterprise Archives; newspaper archives which included the Albany Times Union, Troy Record, Guilderland Library, Schenectady Gazette and others. We thank all of them.

Additional photos that have no identification and not attributed to the photographer but are in the archives of the Altamont Fair are included.

Special thanks to Beverly and her committee for organizing the archives. Apologies to anyone not acknowledged and will be added in future editions.

However, the biggest thank you goes to Pat Canaday who without her leadership and support this book would not have been made possible.

Introduction

For anyone growing up in New York State going to a county fair has always been part of their life experience. For 378 years there has been a public fair of some form starting in 1641 in what is today New York City. For those of us in the Capital District there have been county fairs since the early nineteenth century.

The advantage of living in the Capital District is that several counties surround it and each has their own version of the county fair. For fair aficionados, August and September is "Fair Season" and many of us try to visit each.

However, no matter where you live the Altamont Fair has always been a favorite. Nestled between the Helderberg Escarpment and the Village of Altamont, New York, the Altamont Fair has been entertaining the public for 125 years and this book is a testimony to that century-plus fact.

My own experiences began in the 1960s as a teenager and then later as an adult and particularly as a parent making sure my children enjoyed the rides, the food, and experience ever since. I have not missed going to the Altamont Fair for over 50 years. I have interviewed fair goers who have longer records than that.

This 125th anniversary book features a history of the fair movement in New York State and in the Capital region and particularly the origin of the Altamont Fair. Included is a historical timeline from 1892 to 2018 featuring many newspaper accounts, personal observations, and reports of what each year featured during this timeline. Included also are notes from the minutes of the fair association, the men and woman, and yes even youngsters, who made the decisions each year on how to run the fair, to what forms of entertainment to bring in, day by day decisions on building maintenance, rebuilding or new construction, and the politics of the day. Running a fair takes hundreds of people including paid staff, volunteers, and their labor to insure that the public has a thoroughly enjoyable experience. The COVID Pandemic which started in 2019 and continues to this date has forced us to cover only the years up to 2018.

The best part of the book are the hundreds of photographs that were taken by fair goers, staff, volunteers, professionals, mom and pops, newspapers, and every other possible source. The fair archives are filled with such memories and hundreds of faces, events, and exhibits fill the book. In fact you may even see yourself, your friends, family or relatives enjoying the day at the fair. In the back of the book are pages where you can record your own experiences for the next five years insuring that your memories become part of the Fair's history too!

The Altamont Fair has been bringing city and country together with tradition since 1893. It will do so for many more years to come.

This is the souvenir edition. The collector's edition that is more than 500 pages includes a fair timeline, biographies, and almost 900 illustrations is also available.

Don Rittner
February 2022

2017, Gina Verrelli

The Birth of the County Fair

Ben Franklin said there were two things you can count on — death and taxes. In New York State you can add county fairs. This annual tradition that marks the promotion and celebration of our agricultural heritage has been a tradition that dates back to early Dutch times.

The first fair in what is now New York State began in 1641. An ordinance was passed on September 30 to begin an annual cattle fair in New Amsterdam (present New York City) to begin on October 15 and a hog fair on November 1.

> **ORDINANCE**
>
> Of the Director and Council of New Netherland, establishing an annual Fair at New Amsterdam. *Passed 30th September*, 1641.
> [N. Y. Col. MSS. IV. 131.]
>
> BE it known hereby to all persons, that the Director and Council of *New Netherland* have ordained that henceforth there shall be held annually at *Fort Amsterdam* a Cattle Fair on the 15th of October, and a fair for Hogs on the 1st of November. Whosoever hath any thing to sell or to buy can regulate himself accordingly.
>
> Done 30th September and affixed at said Fort.

The New York Agricultural Fair in 1850 took place in Menands outside of Albany. Painting of the event by John Wilson. Original at the Albany Institute of History and Art.

The Birth of the County Fair

On November 28, 1658, the Burgomaster (mayor) and Schepens (municipal officers) of New Amsterdam (now New York City) passed an ordinance to have two cattle fairs in the city. One for lean cattle on May 1 until the end of the month, and one for fat cattle to begin on October 20 until the end of November. This was to be an annual event.

On November 11, 1692, the New York State Legislature passed a law called *"An act for settling fairs and markets in each respective city and co. throughout this province."* This was the law of the State until it was repealed on March 12, 1788. A special law was passed on March 8, 1773, for fairs in Albany, Cumberland (now part of Vermont), and Tryon (now Montgomery) counties but the American Revolution put a halt to those plans before they could come to fruition.

For years later towns applied for special permission to the State to have agricultural fairs but eventually they turned into more like present day farmers markets. There were no more competitions, winning prizes, and glory and satisfaction for

New York Agricultural Fair in 1850 took place in Menands, NY outside of Albany. Engraving of the event by E. Forbes and Richard H. Pease. Original at the Albany Institute of History and Art.

The Birth of the County Fair

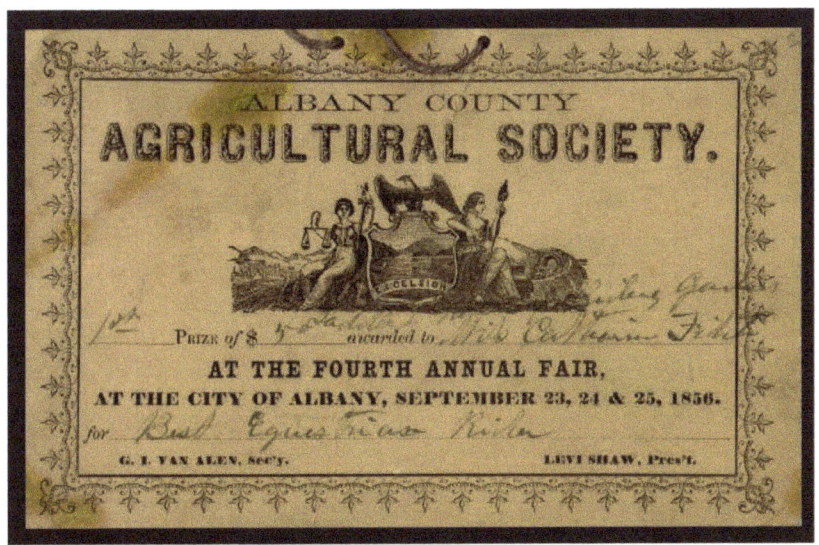

A certificate was awarded to first prize winners at the annual fair in Albany. This one is dated 1856. Source: AIHA.

beating your neighboring farmers in size of vegetables, fruits, or the best looking cattle for the year. They were usually held twice a year.

Things were to change, however. "The Society of The Promotion of Agriculture, Arts, and Manufacturers" was incorporated on March 12, 1793. In 1801, it divided the State into agriculture districts and a secretary was appointed to oversee each one. The Secretary of each district would hold meetings for society members in their respective districts and each year the State Legislature would publish the combined annual transactions of the society. The list of members is a virtual who's who of important people in New York during the eighteenth and early nineteenth centuries: Robert R. Livingston (signer of the Declaration of Independence) was its first president. Others included John Lansing, considered one of the Founding Fathers of the United States of America. He was a delegate to the Constitutional Convention in 1787, at which the U. S. Constitution was adopted and the United States of America was officially formed. Stephen Van Rensselaer was the Patroon of Rensselaerswyck, and Simeon De Witt, who was Geographer and Surveyor General of the Continental Army during the American Revolution and

A certificate was awarded to prize winners at the annual fair. This one is dated 1864. Source: AIHA.

The Birth of the County Fair

Surveyor General of the State of New York for the fifty years from 1784 until his death.

First Premium Award, September 11-14, 1899
(Unidentified recipient)   **R.J. McCauley**, President.

The society's charter expired in 1804 but revived and continued until April 2 under a new name, "The Society for the Promotion of the Useful Arts." It had nine members (Livingston was first president as well) and four annual reports were published by the State. Many of these can be found on the Internet and are interesting reading.

Between 1808 and 1812, $10,000 in premiums were awarded for the best clothes of household manufacture and awarded by the county judge and the society combined. These samples were given and preserved in the Albany Institute, now the Albany Institute of History and Art in Albany, New York.

The society was eventually replaced by a Board of Agriculture in 1819 and State funding was withdrawn, but it continued as a local organization of Albany until it merged with the Albany Lyceum of Natural History (incorporated on April 23, 1828,

Elkanah Watson. Created the first American County Fair in 1810. From Wikipedia.

The Birth of the County Fair

under the presidency of Stephen Van Rensselaer) both of which became part of the Albany Institute which incorporated on February 27, 1829. The members of both the Society for the Promotion of Useful Arts and the Albany Lyceum felt they overlapped in purpose and so joined forces to create the Albany Institute. The present Albany Institute of History and Art is now the result of the merging of the Albany Institute and the Albany Historical and Art Society (1851-1899) in 1900.

The Albany Institute was given the books, papers, and effects of its predecessors for safekeeping.

"An act to improve the agriculture of this state," was passed on April 7, 1819, and created a board of agriculture and allocated $10,000 annually for two years to promote agriculture and family domestic manufactures in several New York counties provided that a match was given by the county societies formed under the law. They met in Albany each year with each county board member who then decided what to have published each year by the State. Three volumes of memoirs were published and the board continued for a little while after the two years.

The Albany County Agricultural Society published and distributed for free an annual "Agricultural Tracts" loaded with tips and articles on agriculture for fair goers. Source: Don Rittner

In 1819, the Albany County Agricultural Society organized the Agricultural Jubilee or Ploughboy's Holiday and was held at the State Capitol and in Washington Park. Source: Don Rittner.

The Birth of the County Fair

County societies were then formed in 1817 based on the plan of the Berkshire County Agriculture Society. These types of societies were promoted by the likes of DeWitt Clinton, Elkanah Watson, and others and lasted for a time but eventually fell into disuse though Jefferson County continued unbroken and continues today to be the longest running county fair in America.

It was Englishman Elkanah Watson from Albany who created the country's first agricultural fair when he moved to the Berkshires. In 1807, he displayed his two prized Merino sheep in Park Square (Pittsfield, Massachusetts) and it garnered quite the crowd and interest. That was the seed of the agricultural fair as we know it. He formed the Berkshire Agricultural Society and they had the first show in 1811. It was called the "Cattle Show" and featured 382 sheep, seven bulls, 109 oxen, nine cows, three heifers, two calves and a boar. He moved back to Albany in 1816.

In February 1832, the "New York State Agricultural Society" was founded in Albany by a group of farmers, legislators, and supporters who wanted nonpartisan support for the advancement of agriculture in the state. The first officers were Le Ray de Chaumont from Jefferson County, President; E. P. Livingston, Jacob Morris, and Robert L. Ross, Vice Presidents; P. S. Van Rensselaer, Recording secretary; Jesse Buel, Corresponding Secretary; Charles R. Webster,

First minutes to create a fair in Altamont in 1892. Source Altamont Fair.

The Birth of the County Fair

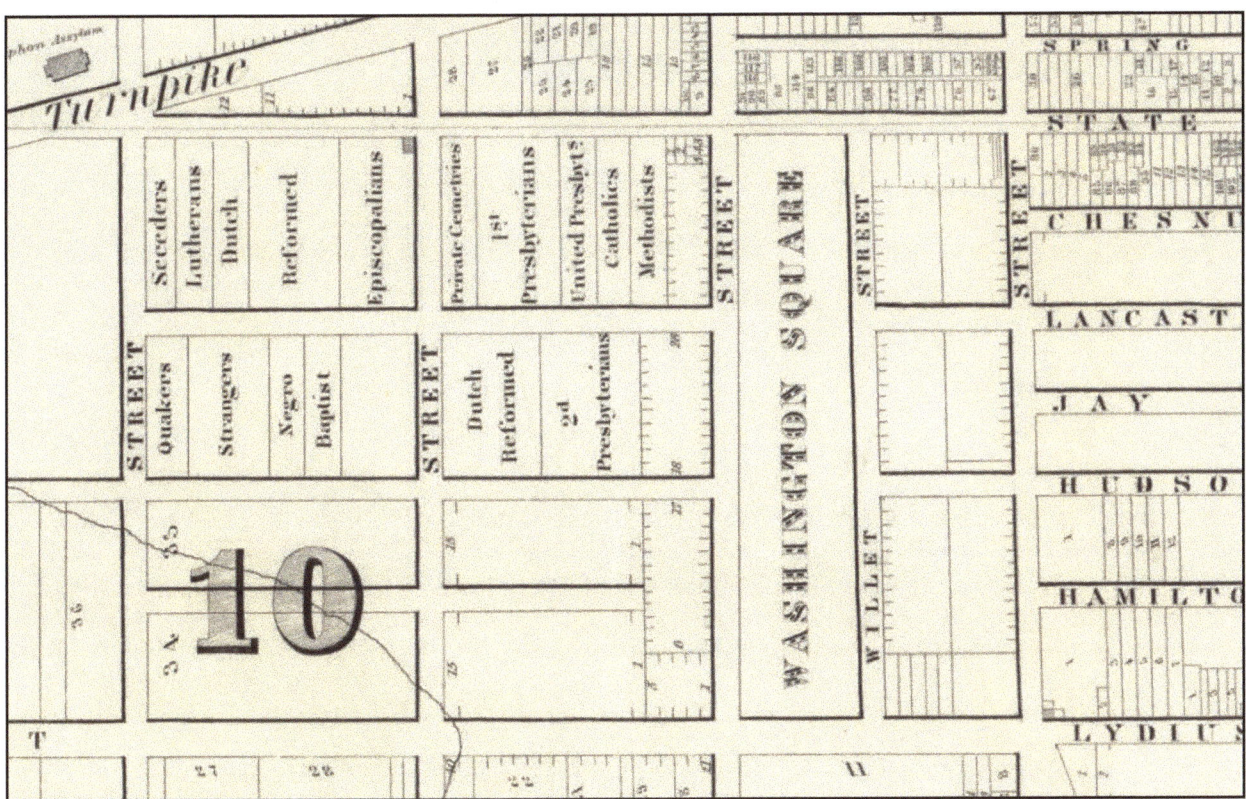

Washington Square (now park). In 1818 the Albany County Agricultural Society received $350 from the State of New York and held three annual fairs. In 1819 it organized the Agricultural Jubilee or Ploughboy's Holiday and was held at the State Capitol and Washington Park (then just a square).

The original Capitol in Albany. Photo Don Rittner.

Treasurer; and H. W. Delavan, John Townsend, and H. Hickox, Executive Committee, were the first officers. History buffs will know some of these names. Under this leadership county societies were formed in many counties with the group's support but again many were short lived.

The Society lobbied for the creation of an agricultural college in 1833 and although turned down repeatedly by the legislature it finally passed in 1865 (now Cornell).

To help promote the society and promote its principles, *The Cultivator*,

The Birth of the County Fair

a magazine/newspaper, was published beginning in March 1834 by Jesse Buell, well known Albany businessman and Apple grower/experimenter. Financed by Stephen Van Rensselaer, the Patroon, and James Wadsworth, it was the official organ of the society and promoter of agriculture among members and the public. Luther Tucker published *The Cultivator*. It merged with *The Genesee Farmer* in 1839 until 1866 when it was merged with *The Country Gentleman*.

For years the society petitioned the State to allow a state wide fair and it was finally granted in 1841 and held in Syracuse that year. The society ran them for the next 60 years, with various cities hosting them, until the Department of Agriculture and Markets obtained the rights in 1899. From 1841 to 1899 the annual *Transactions of the New York Agricultural Society* were published detailing the fairs, winners, and other activities of the society. The State Fair moved

Before Syracuse became the permanent site of the NYS Fair, Albany hosted several times. Source: Internet.

The Birth of the County Fair

around the state and was held in Albany in 1842, 1850, 1859, 1871, 1873, 1876, 1880, 1885, and last in 1889. In 1890, Syracuse became the permanent site.

It made sense that agricultural fairs would be an important part of New York State since New York was the leading agrarian state in the county in the early 19th century.

In 1818 the Albany County Agricultural Society received $350 from the state and held three annual fairs. In 1819 it organized the Agricultural Jubilee or Ploughboy's Holiday and was held at the State Capitol and Washington Park (then just a square) in Albany.

The Albany and Rensselaer Horticultural Society met in the Geological Rooms on State Street (the first US State Museum) in September of 1848 and had fairs in 1849 and 1850. In the meeting rooms of the State Agricultural Society at Albany on Thursday, May 14, 1853, several people met to create an Albany County Agricultural Society. The first fair was held in Bethlehem Corners on October 4-6, 1853, and only raised $900. There was a

In the meeting rooms of the State Agricultural Society at Albany on Thursday, May 14, 1853, several people met to create a county agricultural society.

The Birth of the County Fair

Panorama of Altamont by Lucien Burleigh in 1890. The fair ground is in the upper left. Source: Library of Congress.

historic marker placed at the site (NYS 32, 100 Yd. SW of US 9W, Bethlehem, NY, USA. Latitude & Longitude: 42° 37′ 5.4768″, -73° 47′ 5.7264″). This was near the present Route 9/Route 32 split in Glenmont. The marker is now gone. It was too far from the city and no way to get to it. In 1854 they moved it to the Washington Parade Grounds in Albany on Sept. 25-27. The following years saw it moved to various locales: 1856 to Washington Parade Grounds; 1857 in Albany; 1858, Washington Parade Grounds; 1859-60 both in Albany. No fair was held in 1861.

First NYS Museum (Geological Rooms) on State Street in Albany.

On March 16, 1862, it was reorganized as the Town Union Agricultural Association of the County of Albany and on June 7, 1862, changed its name to the Albany County Agricultural Society. Again from 1863 and 1864 the parade grounds was the fair grounds but in 1865 it moved to Island Park (Menands) and a joint fair was held with the Rensselaer County Agricultural and Manufacturers' Society fair.

The Birth of the County Fair

The society continued to have fairs and in 1873 the Albany Agricultural and Art Association was formed. They purchased 44 acres of land four miles north of the city between the Watervliet turnpike (present Broadway) and horse railway on the East and the Albany and Saratoga Railroad on the West. It was designed by John Bogart. It was here that The New York State Agricultural Society held its State Fair in 1873.

The Move to Altamont

A public meeting was held in Altamont on August 6, 1892, in the house of J. O. Switt and a five person committee, consisting of J. Reamer, Sanford Becker, George J. Williamson, M. R. Hellenbeck and James Keenholts, and was formed to investigate the possibility of hosting an annual fair in Altamont and to raise stock. State aid was given to the fair. On September 3, in the house of J. O. Stitt, a motion was made by W. Hilton and Jacob VanAernam for volunteers to go to the Cobleskill County Agricultural Society fair and report back. The Altamont Enterprise wrote: *"The question of the benefits of a fair of this kind, are undisputed. The financial success, when properly conducted, are assured. Our location, with the handsome amount already subscribed for an object of this kind, are unsurpassed. Shall we have it?"*

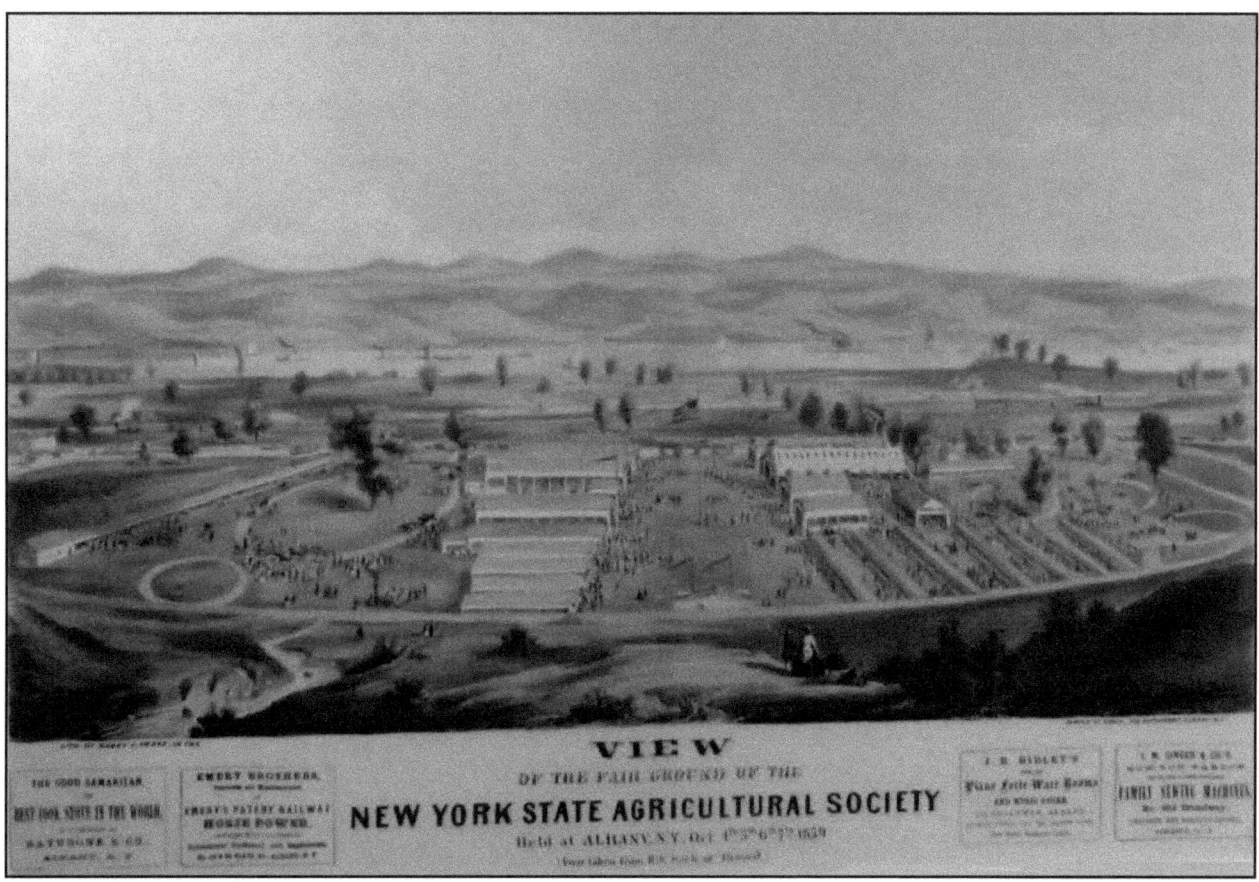

In 1859, the NYS Fair was held for the third time in Albany.

The Birth of the County Fair

The fair was initially a stockholder fair with 200 subscriptions needed. The present Fine Arts building was the first building built at the fair and was built in 1896. The other two old buildings are the gateway building at the foot of Grand Street and the original Grandstand building.

In 1893 the Albany County Fair moved to present Altamont and held its first fair on September 12-15. It was well attended.

In 1922 the fair became the Schenectady-Albany County Fair. In 1926 most of the concessions were Schenectady based merchants. The attendance record for that day, on September 1, 1926, saw 35,000 paid admissions. There were 5,000 exhibitors.

In 1945 Greene County joined and it became the Albany, Schenectady and Green County Fair Association, the only three county fair in the state.

Before Syracuse became the permanent site of the NYS Fair, Albany hosted it several times.

The Grange Movement and the Altamont Fair

The farm community association known as the Grange is an important part of the Altamont Fair. According to one history, the Grange was born out of the end of the Civil War in an effort to heal the wounds of warfare and restore

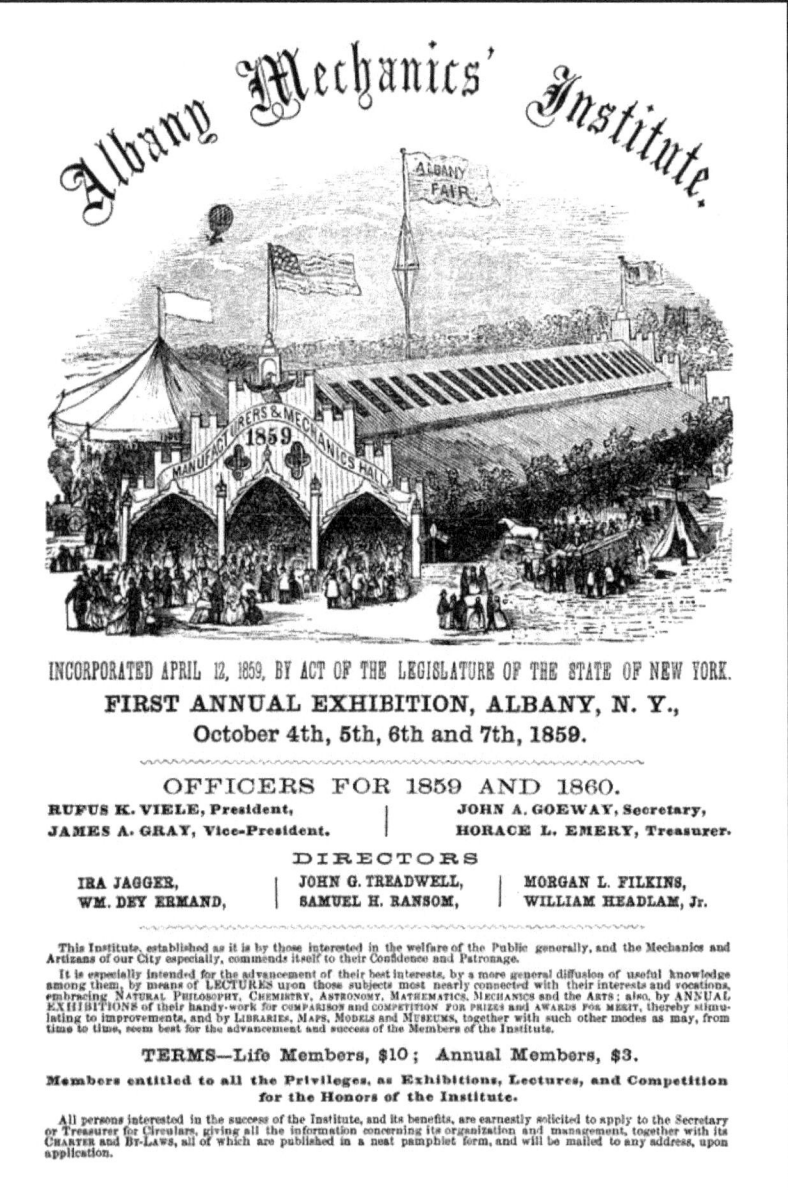

The Albany Mechanics' Institute had its first fair in 1859.

normal conditions of the devastated parts of the South. Oliver Hudson Kelley originated the idea to create a national agricultural society that would educate farmers in the 1850s. As a result of his fact finding mission to the South, commissioned by President Johnson, he decided that this new organization should be a fraternity to aid in healing the war wounds from both the North and South, and establishing it should be a priority. Kelley and William Saunders, a landscape artist from Washington D. C. who was the superintendent of the government's experimental gardens and grounds in D. C., are considered the most significant of the seven founders of the Grange. Francis Marion McDowell, the only founder who was not a D. C. resident was a prominent fruit grower in Steuben County, NY. The first formal meeting of the Grange founders took place on November 15, 1867. It was formally organized on December 4, 1867, and considered the birthday of the Grange.

By 1875 there were over 762,263 members of the Grange fraternity. New York State had 11,723 members.

The New York State Grange was founded in 1873 and incorporated on May 21, 1874. One of the important features of the Grange was that it gave equal access to woman on its councils and was an early supporter of woman's suffrage. It was against liquor traffic, favoring prohibition, and raised relief for fellow members in the West when grasshoppers devastated crops in that part of the country. The Grange created the first life insurance company in 1874 by creating the Patron's Aid a mutual assessment company but abandoned it due to lack of support.

Around 1900, Grange Day was established at the New York State Fair. Between 1874 and 1943, 38 Granges in Albany, Schenectady and Greene Counties were formed.

Many of the local Granges participate in the Altamont Fair as volunteers and by having their own educational exhibits and contests among member granges. The Grange is an integral part of the annual fair.

Summary

Throughout the years at the fair grounds buildings were erected, modified, moved and removed as the fair expanded to meet the needs of a changing society and their desire for entertainment. While the focus was always on the rural agricultural community as a place to congregate once a year, the fair goers saw the introduction of horse racing, chariot racing, auto racing, demolition derby and special auto daredevils until the grandstand burned down in 1995.

The Birth of the County Fair

The decline in farming in the county was showcased when a farm museum was created in 1963. Here fair goers could see farm machinery of the past, many still operating.

The auto races were under the charge of the Eastern Speedway Association and had the sanction of AAA (American Automotive Association) officials. Many well-known racers from around the country participated in the Altamont races. Records were made and broken. Joie Chitwood and his auto daredevils always put on a show with ramp-to-ramp jumps, head crashes and rollovers each year. Altamont's own Lee Wallard won the famed Indianapolis 500 race in 1951 with his Number 99 Belanger Special to victory, at age 40. The following year he appeared at Altamont.

Harness racing was a big hit at the fair from the earliest years until the judge's stand was removed in 1955. It was a staple of the fair for over 50 years. The year 1939 was the highlight of horse racing as Billy Direct paced the mile at 2:01 ¼. That was a new record for the half-mile track. Vic Fleming, trainer of the great horse that went on to establish a world's record of 1:55 on a mile track, drove Billy Direct, that day.

It is safe to say many thousands of fair goers went through the turnstiles over the course of a century and a half at Altamont. The highest fair attendance in a single years was in 1985 with 130,824.

In 1945 it became the only Tri-County Fair in the state when Greene County was added to Albany and Schenectady counties. It continues to be the only Tri-County Fair. In 1955 it was the third largest attended fair in the entire state.

Music has always been an integral part of the fair and it has seen almost every form of music presented, as well as record hops and even battle of the bands where rock and rollers competed. Old Songs Festival, a music institution for years moved to the Fairgrounds in 1982 and built the Dutch Barn. Celebrity acts performed. Some were rising stars, while others were making a comeback. Even exhibits came and went. For years railroad engines of bygone years and a model railroad exhibit were popular but were replaced to make room for a changing public taste. A new fire fighting museum and an auto museum were created for example.

Governors gave speeches and TV personalities appeared. Many local businesses displayed their new products. Food concessions were plentiful and the Midway

The Birth of the County Fair

was supplied by a number of companies such as the Coleman Brothers, Bernardi Greater Shows, Bruce Greater Shows, Reithoffer, and the O. C. Buck Shows featuring not only the expected Ferris wheel but even the latest high tech rides in recent years. Circus performers were always a big hit with trapeze stunts, horse riding, clowns, and circus animals performing their tricks. Youngsters could see zebras, giraffe's and other exotic animals.

Starting in 1967 and continuing each year a Miss Altamont Fair is crowned showcasing a local young woman who displays her talents, answers questions, and models formal wear for the judges. Seventeen-year-old Cohoes native Deborah Jan Murray was crowned the first Queen of the Altamont Fair. Winners perform a great deal of community service projects during their reign.

It isn't a fair without the 4-H'ers showing what they made and the local Grange Halls, an important institution for the farmer, putting on their demonstrations and providing services.

But the core mission of the county fair was not ignored. Scores of horses, cattle, sheep, pigs, goats, chickens all competed for money and ribbons. Little ones could watch baby chickens hatch, goats, calves and foals being born, or sheep being sheared. There were tractor pulls, milking demonstrations, and the latest farm implements displayed to make the farmer a little more productive in the field.

The fair did not ignore the social issues of the time. There were suffragette stands, model nuclear fallout shelters, model homes of the future (A Gold Medallion Electric home), health issues of the day, and even a State Attorney General consumer fraud booth, for example.

The fair survived inclement weather, power loses, lightning strikes, hurricanes and even tornadoes. "The Show Must Go On" certainly lived up to its reputation over the years.

And so every year the Altamont Fair attempts to bring in new forms of entertainment while showcasing their permanent exhibits. Like any venue it will continue to change with the times and needs of the community it serves. It has been doing this successfully for 125 years and will continue for the next century and more creating memories that will be shared forever.

The Birth of the County Fair

The Birth of the County Fair

Photo Gallery
Altamont Fair Over the Centuries

Thousands of families from all over the Capital District and elsewhere have flocked to the Altamont Fair over the last 125 years. They have been entertained, educated, won prizes, developed friendships, saw animals and competitions, and simply had a good time. Here is just a sample of photographs taken over the years. Many of the photos were taken by fair workers, general public, local newspapers and unknown people that have ended up in the archives of the Fair's headquarters. When known, the dates are given and captions are provided with information that was placed on the photograph. There are photos that date back from the first fair in 1893 to modern times. If you are able to identify any person or event, please contact the author at drittner@aol.com, so it can be included in revisions of the book.

Old Grandstand in 1893 now the Poultry Barn (first floor).

Early Carousel

Early view of the fairground with original buildings and track, 1890s.

Early Ferris Wheel in the early 1900s held few seats. Courtesy: Albany Times Union. The Ferris Wheel was invented by an RPI Graduate in Troy, NY named George Ferris.

Miss Altamont Fair.

For a quarter ride a stagecoach.

1959

Rodeos were introduced in the 1920s

Billy Direct in 1939. He established a new track record at Altamont of 2:01 1/4. Harold Han.

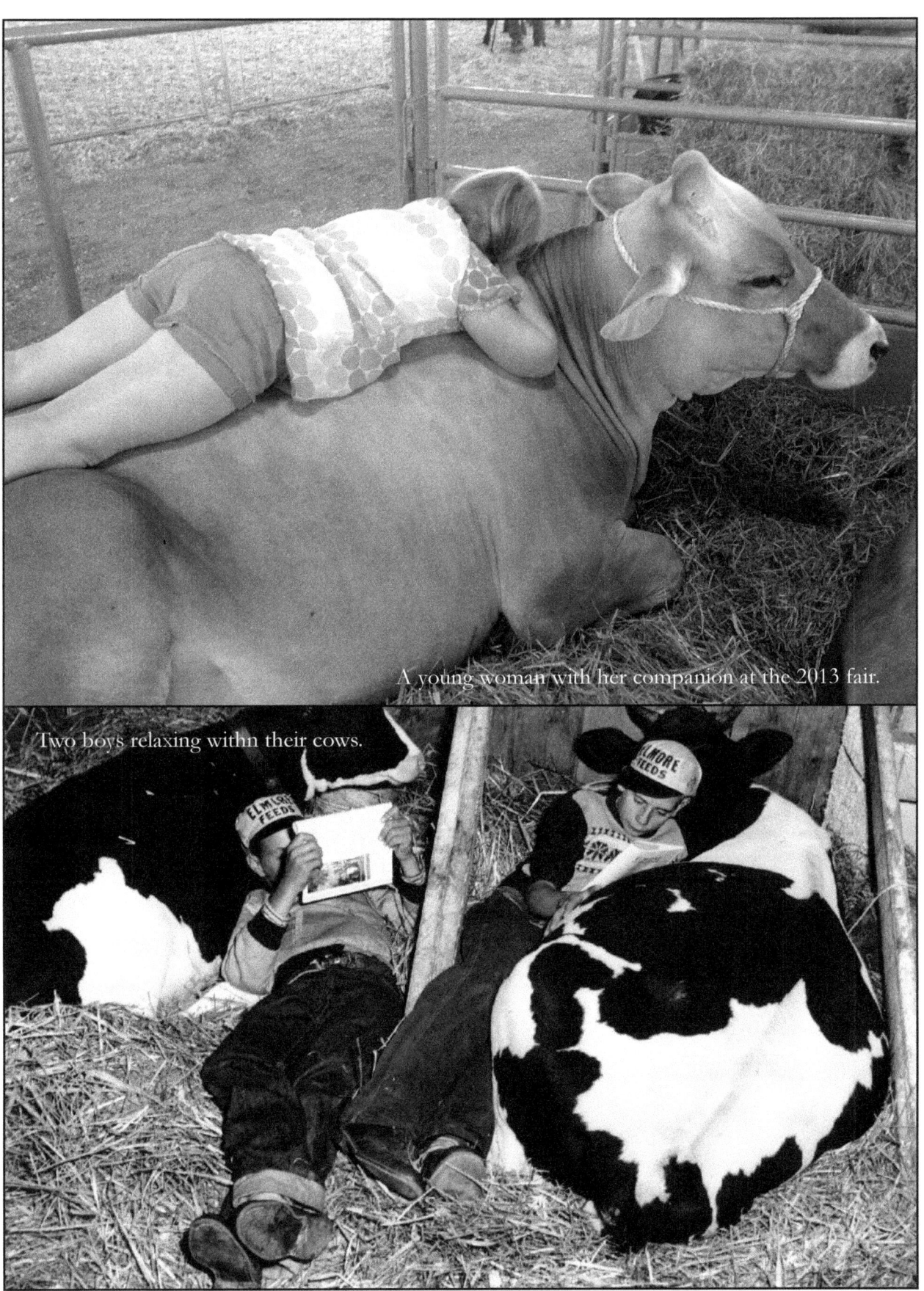

A young woman with her companion at the 2013 fair.

Two boys relaxing withn their cows.

The last demolition derby took place in 1995. The grandstand burned down in November. It was decided not to rebuild the grandstand making racing come to an end since the beginning of the fair at Altamont.

Auto races began at the fair in 1927.

Lee Wallard began his racing career in 1935 on the dirt track at fairgrounds around the Northeast, including the Altamont Fairgrounds starting in 1938. He ran 64 races from 1941 to 1951 but only won six times. In 1951, he won the Indianapolis 500. Courtesy of the Village of Altamont Archives & Museum The Edwin Bradt Collection.

Elmer Davis of Poughkeepsie raced in the 1950 fair which saw six accidents that year at the fairground. Here his car on the right flips but he walked out of it unhurt.

Joie Chitwood started his race car driving career in 1934 at a dirt track in Winfield, Kansas. From there, he began racing sprint cars. In 1939 and 1940 he won the AAA East Coast Sprint car championship. His thrill show lasted more than 40 years and he appeared on TV and was a stunt coordinator for movies. His sons continued after he retired. Courtesy of the Village of Altamont Archives & Museum The Edwin Bradt Collection.

Bob Sall was a popular and winning driver in Altamont during the mid 1930s.

G.W. Hockaday, 1980

Left to right: Paola Painter, Neal Taber, Midge Peterson, John Armstrong, and Cindy Pollard.

There was an oxen pulled bandwagon in 1977.

The Miss Altamont Fair begain in 1967.

The 1960s saw rockets, jets, and even a nine story Atlas Missile.

Bicycle Race

1893. At that fair there was a half-mile bicycle race for women for which the First Prize was a pair of diamond earrings valued at $175.

Sack Race

1964. A Gold Medallion Home, a new all electric ranch style home constructed on the fairground was on exhibit all week. The house and lot on Fairview Avenue was given away on Saturday night to Mr. and Mrs. David J. Richards of Colonie.

1992, Don Rittner

Sue Clark

Fairgoers enjoying a daredevil stunts like this one in 1956.

D&H #4122 and Caboose at the fair.

TV Star Gabby Hayes entertained kids during the 1957 fair. He was the sidekick to Hopalong Cassidy Boyd, Gene Autry, John Wayne, Roy Rogers and others.

Fire breathing lady at 2010 Altamont Fair. Photo by Sue Clark.

August 8, 1983. Resting clowns.

In 1970 there were two Ferris Wheels to entertain. Courtesy Albany Times Union.

High Flying Act in 1962.

Youngsters waiting in line for the Tilt-A-Whirl at the 1960 fair.

Young lady admiring the ladies homemade clothing at the 1959 fair.

Aerial view of the fairgrounds in 1954.

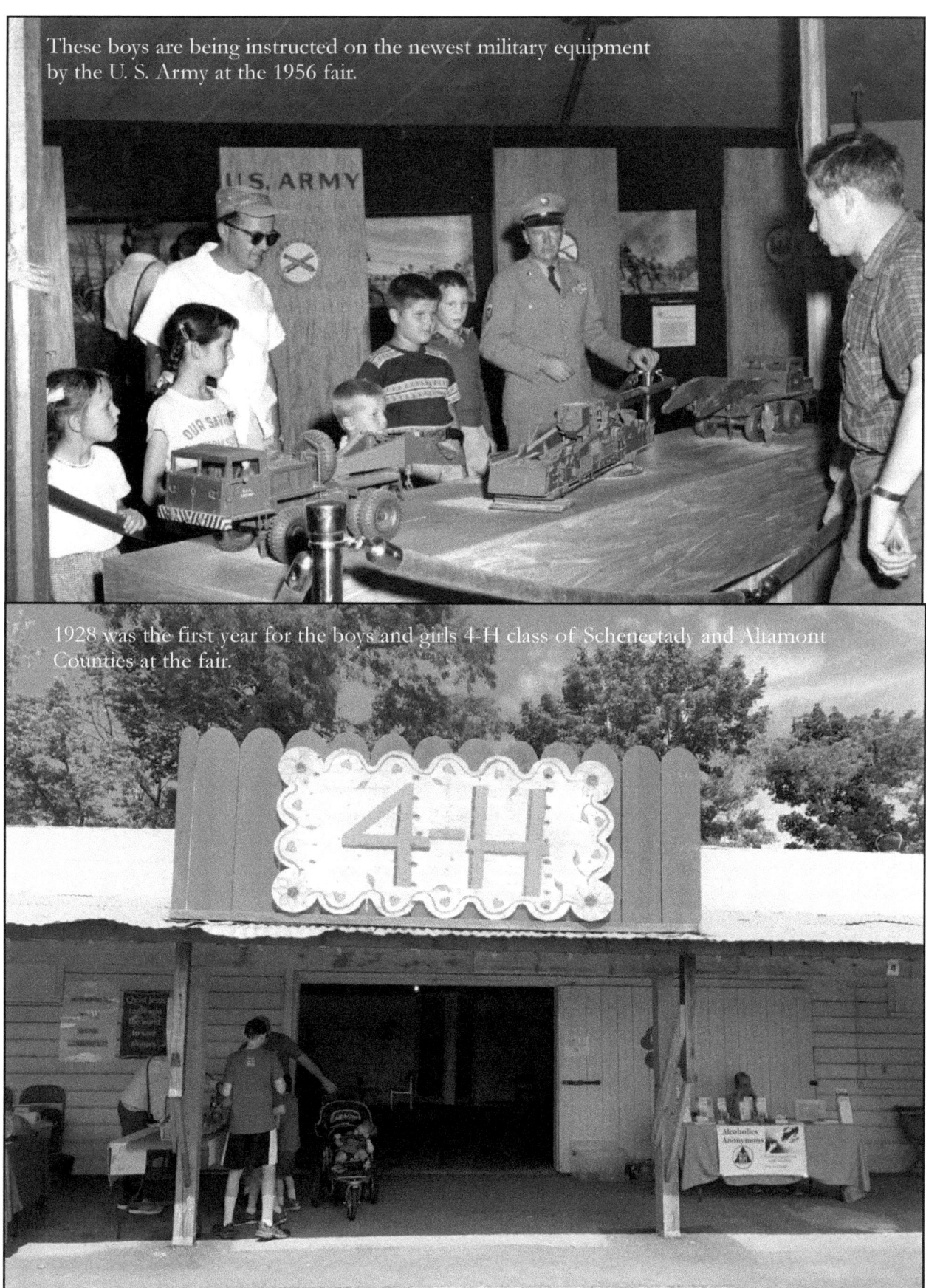

These boys are being instructed on the newest military equipment by the U. S. Army at the 1956 fair.

1928 was the first year for the boys and girls 4-H class of Schenectady and Altamont Counties at the fair.

Circus Hollywood had seven acts under the Big Top.

2016, Don Rittner

Governor Nelson Rockefeller speaking to the crowd in 1960.

NYS Governor James B. O'Dell (left) visits the fair in 1903 Standing left Gov. O'Dell, right James Keenholts, President of the fair. Seated left to right: Montford A. Sand (bald), Fred Keenholts, Jr., Secty; Hiram Griggs (bearded); Mr. Wilbur (Oneonta) last seated near Govenor Edward Becker.

There were 41 entries in the 1951 Memorial Day midget auto races, members of the American Racing Driver's Club.

The Crowd looks on at the races.

Chitwood's Hell Drivers, a troupe of stunt drivers thrilled visitors. Top left to bottom: Stage show; Joie Chitwood made this car roll over twice over a ramp on two wheels; Chitwood and Gibson smashing four cars. Top right to bottom: After 4 cars have smashed; Chitwood smashing a car up; and Gibson moving through a wooden boarder of fire. C. 1934.

1961

Helicopter rides were given.

Car races were popular for many years at the Fair.

Horse Races which began around 1901 were always a big hit.

Mary Blackstone, of Schenectady was a popular Trotter and horse driver during the early 1960s with her horse named Prince.

Coleman's Midway was popular in the 1930s.

Your Memories

My Memories

Favorite Events

Favorite Photo

Favorite Food

Favorite Ride

Did You Win A Prize?

The Weather?

Describe your Experience

Your Memories

My Memories

Favorite Events

Favorite Photo

Favorite Food

Favorite Ride

Did You Win A Prize?

The Weather?

Describe your Experience

www.ingramcontent.com/pod-product-compliance
Lightning Source LLC
Chambersburg PA
CBHW060936170426
43194CB00026B/2973